FAMOUS EVENTS
AND SYMBOLS OF AMERICA

LEVEL  READER

READING
GRADES 2 TO 4
3
LEVEL

Written by Bethany Snyder and Kathryn Knight
Illustrated by Laurance Cleyet-Merle

bendon®

© Bendon, Inc. All rights reserved.
The BENDON name and logo are trademarks
of Bendon, Inc., Ashland, OH 44805

THE FOUNDING OF JAMESTOWN

Can you imagine being one of the first settlers in America? In 1607, three ships full of English men and boys landed in Virginia to start a silkworm farm. They settled on a river and called their new home Jamestown, after King James of England.

The settlers faced many troubles, hunger, and disease. They were not prepared for the hard work of starting a colony in a strange new land.

After years of struggle, the colony grew as settlers began to trade with the Native Americans and learn to grow crops. Jamestown became the first permanent settlement in America.

DID YOU KNOW?

One of the most important men in Jamestown was Captain John Smith. He was captured by the Native Americans but was later rescued by the chief's young daughter, Pocahontas.

THE FIRST THANKSGIVING

In 1620, a group of 102 people sailed from England to America in a ship called the *Mayflower*. They wanted a better life and freedom to worship as they chose. They were Puritans, also known as Pilgrims. They landed in what is now Massachusetts and called their new settlement Plymouth.

Life in the new world was not easy. With the help of Native Americans Squanto and Samoset, they learned how to plant crops. The next year, 52 Pilgrims and 90 Native American friends celebrated their survival with a three-day harvest feast—with seafood, turkey, deer, vegetables, and fruits. This became known as the First Thanksgiving.

DID YOU KNOW?
In 1863, President Lincoln proclaimed that a day be set aside each year for thanksgiving and praise. "Turkey Day" is celebrated the fourth Thursday of November.

THE BOSTON TEA PARTY

A late-night tea party kicked off the American Revolution! It took place on December 16, 1773. That night, dozens of American colonists, some disguised as Mohawk Indians, dumped chests full of English tea into Boston harbor.

Why? The colonists were angry that England was charging a tax on tea. The colonists could not vote, and they had no voice in English government. Should they be forced to pay English taxes? The Sons of Liberty said "No!" They rebelled against the unfair tax by dumping the tea in the water!

DID YOU KNOW?

342 crates of tea were dumped into the harbor that night. That is over 10,000 pounds of tea—about as heavy as an elephant!

SIGNING THE DECLARATION OF INDEPENDENCE

After many years of British control, the Colonies wanted to get out from under the rule of the "crown." They did not like being taxed and punished by a king who did not listen to them.

This group of Americans wrote a very polite but clear paper explaining why they should be free to make their own laws. Thomas Jefferson wrote that God had granted all men the right to "life, liberty, and the pursuit of happiness," and that *no* ruler could take those rights away. The paper was dated July 4, 1776, and used the words "United States of America" for the very first time!

DID YOU KNOW?

John Hancock signed his name very large so the King of England wouldn't have to put on his glasses to read it!

OUR FLAG

If you could design a flag, what would it look like? The American colonists wanted their own flag, since they did not want to be ruled by England. On June 14, 1777, they chose the design. It had 13 stripes and 13 stars, to stand for the 13 colonies. The stripes were red and white, and the white stars were on a blue square.

Now our flag has 50 stars, one for each state. We are very proud of our flag, a symbol of our nation. Its nickname is "Old Glory," and we celebrate Flag Day every June 14th.

DID YOU KNOW?

The Pledge of Allegiance honors the flag: "I pledge allegiance to the Flag of the United States of America, and to the Republic for which it stands, one Nation under God, indivisible, with liberty and justice for all."

INDEPENDENCE DAY

How do you celebrate the Fourth of July? Some people march in parades. Some have picnics or watch fireworks.

Do you know why we celebrate on that day? It is a very special holiday. It is our Independence Day. On that day in 1776, America declared itself free from England with the Declaration of Independence.

The first Fourth of July celebration was 1777. Now, every year we celebrate our country's freedom—with family, food, fireworks, and fun!

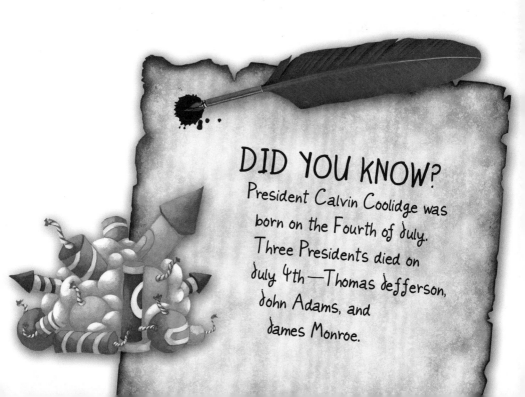

DID YOU KNOW?

President Calvin Coolidge was born on the Fourth of July. Three Presidents died on July 4th—Thomas Jefferson, John Adams, and James Monroe.

OUR CONSTITUTION

"We the people of the United States..."

After the Revolutionary War, our new country needed a plan of government, or Constitution. In 1787, men from several colonies met to write out how our government would be run by the States, the President, and a Supreme Court of judges. Our Constitution was approved on June 21, 1788.

The first ten additions, or Amendments, are called the Bill of Rights. They guaranteed freedoms to every citizen. Other Amendments have been added as our lawmakers work to improve our laws, "...in order to form a more perfect Union."

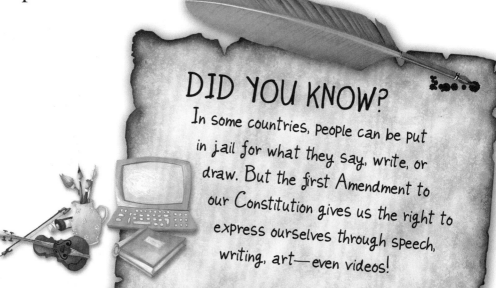

DID YOU KNOW?

In some countries, people can be put in jail for what they say, write, or draw. But the first Amendment to our Constitution gives us the right to express ourselves through speech, writing, art—even videos!

THE LIBERTY BELL

America's most important bell is not rung anymore—because it is cracked! The Liberty Bell was ordered in 1751 to "Proclaim Liberty throughout the land." It was hung in the State House (now Independence Hall) in Philadelphia, Pennsylvania, and rung on important days. The most important ringing was on July 8, 1776, for the first public reading of the Declaration of Independence.

The bell cracked a bit each time it was rung. The crack widened even more when the bell was rung on George Washington's birthday in 1846. The crack is now 2 feet 4 inches long, so every July 4th the bell is tapped instead of rung.

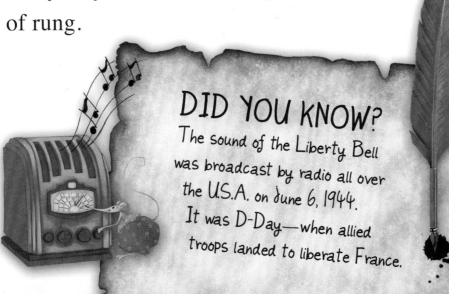

DID YOU KNOW?
The sound of the Liberty Bell was broadcast by radio all over the U.S.A. on June 6, 1944. It was D-Day—when allied troops landed to liberate France.

THE WHITE HOUSE

One of the most famous addresses in the world is 1600 Pennsylvania Avenue. This is where you'll find the White House, home of the President of the United States. It is the oldest government building in Washington, DC, the nation's capital city. This well-known symbol is shown on the back of the twenty-dollar bill. John Adams, the second President, was the first President to live there.

During the War of 1812, the British tried to burn the White House, but the stone walls built in 1792 still stand. Between 5,000 and 6,000 people visit the White House each day.

DID YOU KNOW?
It takes 570 gallons of paint to cover the outside of the White House. President Theodore Roosevelt named it "the White House" in 1901.

EAST MEETS WEST

On May 10, 1869, a very important event took place that changed our nation forever. On this day, a golden spike joined two rails of a railroad track at Promontory Summit in the Utah Territory.

One set of rails had been built running from the east. The other had started in California. When the two tracks met, this linked the entire nation for the first time—from sea to shining sea! The "last spike" of this Transcontinental Railroad was pounded into place in front of a cheering crowd.

DID YOU KNOW?
In 1956, construction began on the Interstate Highway System, linking east, west, north, and south of our big, big land!

New York

San Francisco

THE STATUE OF LIBERTY

In 1885, the United States received a huge gift—the Statue of Liberty. It was from France to honor their long friendship since the American Revolution.

The statue was made in France by the sculptor Frederic-Auguste Bartholdi and the engineer Gustave Eiffel. It was shipped to New York in 350 pieces! Then it was put back together on a tall pedestal on Liberty Island in New York Harbor.

Lady Liberty stands for freedom and democracy. The seven spikes on her crown stand for the seven continents and seven oceans of the world. The tablet reads: July 4, 1776—our Independence Day!

DID YOU KNOW?

The original "face" of Lady Liberty was a copy of Frederic Bartholdi's mother.

THE BALD EAGLE

What's majestic, strong, and found on many American coins and bills? The eagle! The eagle is also on the Great Seal of the United States, holding an olive branch in one talon and arrows in the other. On June 20, 1782, the colonies decided that the eagle was the perfect symbol for America to represent freedom.

DID YOU KNOW?

In 1961, John F. Kennedy wrote: "The fierce beauty and proud independence of this great bird aptly symbolizes the strength and freedom of America."